BUDDIES

BLAZE

BUD

CONTENTS

Wherever you see this sign, ask an adult to help you.

BUDDIES
TELL ME WHY PLANES HAVE WINGS

SHIRLEY WILLIS

Macdonald Young Books

CAN I FLY?

FLYING LOOKS EASY!

You cannot fly because the force of gravity pulls you down.

6

In order to fly,
the force of gravity
has to be overcome.

Birds, bats and
insects can fly
because they can
overcome gravity.

BUZZ

BUZZ

7

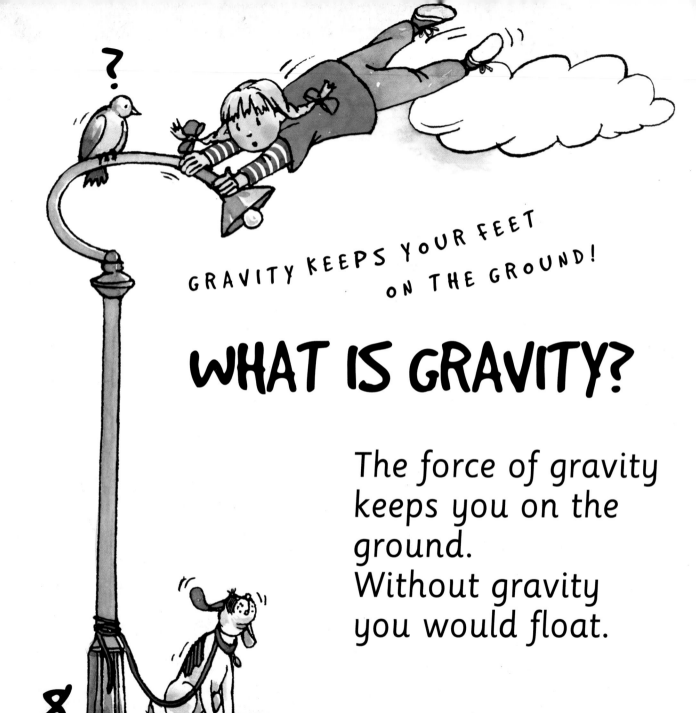

GRAVITY KEEPS YOUR FEET ON THE GROUND!

WHAT IS GRAVITY?

The force of gravity keeps you on the ground.
Without gravity you would float.

8

When something falls – like this apple – it is being pulled downwards by gravity.

BOING!

You cannot see gravity but it pulls everything towards the centre of the Earth.

9

How Do BIRDS FLY?

Birds can fly because they can overcome gravity.

A bird's body is not heavy
so it is easy to lift.
By flapping its wings
a bird is lifted
off the ground
and starts to fly.

10

A bird's body is built
for flying.
It has strong muscles
to flap its wings.
It has hollow bones
and a feather coat to
keep its body light.
This helps a bird
to fly.

11

CAN YOU STOP GRAVITY?

READY, STEADY GO!

You cannot stop gravity but air can slow down its effect.

A PAPER RACE

Take two sheets of paper.
Crumple one sheet into a ball.
Now drop them both together from the same height.

The paper ball falls faster because it is smaller.
The sheet traps more air underneath it.
This slows it down as it falls.

12

How To Make A Parachute

You will need:

A plastic bag
Scissors
A ruler
4 pieces of string
(each 30cm long)
Sticky tape
Plasticine

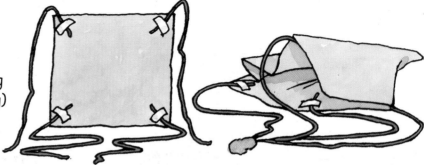

1 With help from an adult, cut a 30cm square from a plastic bag.

2 Tape a piece of string to each corner, as shown.

3 Knot the loose ends together and press into a blob of plasticine.

When an object falls, air can act like a brake to slow it down.

This is called drag.

When a parachute fills with air, it is drag that slows it down.

13

WHAT IS AIR?

Air is an invisible gas
that is all around us.

When air moves from
one place to another
it is called wind.

Wind is moving air.

Warm air rises and cold air sinks.
As the cold air sinks it rushes
into the empty space below.
This is wind.

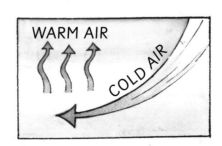

WARM AIR

COLD AIR

You cannot see wind
but you can feel it
blowing against you.
On a windy day
you can see it
blowing trees, windmills
and washing on lines.

15

Do PLANES FLOAT IN THE AIR?

A glider is a plane without an engine.

YOU CAN SEE GLIDERS BUT YOU CAN'T HEAR THEM

Gliders float upwards on rising currents of warm air called thermals.

A glider pilot must follow warm air thermals to stay in the air.

16

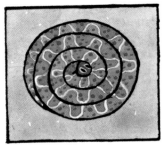  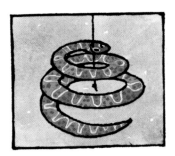

DOES WARM AIR REALLY RISE?

You will need: A sheet of stiff paper
Scissors
A pencil
Some wool
Felt-tip pens

1   Draw a spiral on the paper.
Now colour it to
look like a snake.
2   With help from an adult,
cut around the spiral.
3   Now thread the wool
through the snake's head.
Knot it underneath.

Now hang your snake above
a radiator and watch it spin.
Rising warm air is making it
turn.

17

DO YOU NEED WINGS TO FLY?

Planes, birds, bats and insects all need wings to fly.
But you can fly without wings in a hot-air balloon.

Bubbles rise because they are full of warm air. As the air inside begins to cool, the bubbles start to fall.

Hot air rises because it is lighter than cold air.
A hot-air balloon will float upwards if the air inside it is heated.

19

WHY DO PLANES HAVE WINGS?

A plane needs wings to fly.

When a plane speeds
along a runway,
air rushes past.
As the air rushes
over and under the wings
it lifts the plane.

The upward force
is called lift.

20

A plane's wings are flat underneath and curved on top.
This shape is called an aerofoil.
This special shape lifts the wings and pulls the plane upwards.

WE NEED AEROFOIL-SHAPED ARMS!

21

How Do PLANES STAY UP?

IT'S TIME FOR LIFT OFF!

The lift of
a plane's wings
pulls it up
into the sky
and keeps it there.

WHOOSH!

Engines propel a plane forward at great speed. This is called thrust. If a plane stopped moving forward it would quickly drop from the sky.

HOW TO MAKE A PAPER PLANE

1 Fold a sheet of paper in half.

2 Now fold towards the centre as shown.

3 Fold towards the centre again.

4 Now fold the wings back.

5 It's time for take-off!

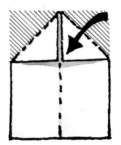

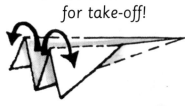

How Do Planes Go So Fast?

A plane needs an engine to go fast.

24

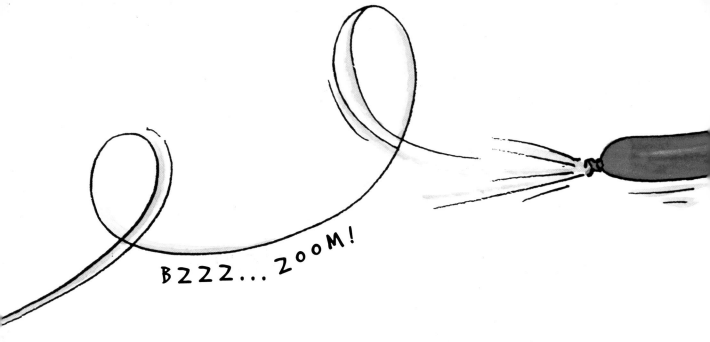

BZZZ... ZOOM!

A JET-PROPELLED BALLOON

Blow up a balloon and let it go.
A jet of air shoots out and
propels the balloon
through the air.

Jet engines make planes go very fast.
A blast of gas rushes from the back
of a jet engine and thrusts the plane
forward at great speed.

25

How Do You Steer A Plane?

A pilot turns his plane by tilting its rudder left or right. He raises or lowers special flaps on the wings and tailplanes to go up or down.

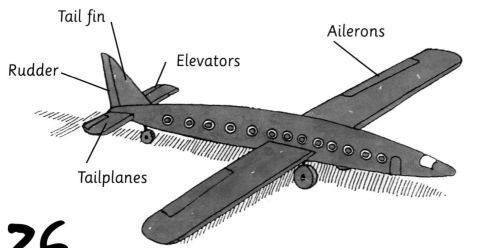

Tail fin

Ailerons

Rudder

Elevators

Tailplanes

The wing flaps are called ailerons. The flaps on the tailplanes are called elevators.

27

CAN PLANES FLY BACKWARDS?

A helicopter can fly backwards or forwards. It can also fly up, down or sideways.

Spin the stick quickly between your hands and flip it into the air. Watch the whirligig fly.

28

HOW TO MAKE A WHIRLIGIG

You will need:

A plastic bottle
A thin stick
Scissors
A felt-tip pen
A ruler

1 Measure out a rectangle (21cm x 3cm) on a plastic bottle. Now cut it out.
2 Mark the middle of the rectangle. Cut a slit on either side, as shown.
3 Make a hole in the middle just big enough to push the stick through.
4 Press the blades down slightly, as shown.

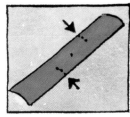

Helicopters have spinning rotor blades instead of wings.
The spinning blades lift the helicopter straight up into the air on take-off.

29

GLOSSARY

aerofoil   A special shape, that creates an upwards force called lift. Helicopter blades and aeroplane wings are aerofoil-shaped.

ailerons   Movable flaps on a plane's wings that help it move up or down.

elevators   Movable flaps on the tailplanes that help a plane to move up or down.

gravity   The downward pull of the Earth.

helicopter   An aircraft that has spinning blades instead of wings for flying.

hot-air balloon   A huge balloon that is filled with hot air to make it rise.

jet engine   An aircraft engine that thrusts hot gases backwards.

lift   An upwards force that overcomes the pull of gravity.

parachute   A device that balloons out like an umbrella as it falls through the air. It helps people land safely on the ground.

plane   An aeroplane, a flying machine with wings.

propel   To make something move forward.

rudder   A movable flap on a plane's tail fin to make it turn left or right.

tail-fin   The upright fin at the back of a plane.

tailplanes   The small back wings of a plane.

thermals   Currents of rising warm air used by gliders to fly upwards.

thrust   The force from the engines which propels a plane through the air.